SO-BCA-900

CHRISTIANCY ELEMENTARY SCHOOL

Consultant on this book—
Dr. Paul Witty, Director
Psycho-Educational Clinic
Northwestern University

The "I Want to Be" books are designed to encourage independent reading on beginner level. The concepts—broad as a child's imagination—bring pleasure to early reading experience and better understanding of the world. But the text is in line with the young reader's new skill.

All but ten of the one-hundred-eighty-eight words of the vocabulary used in this book are from the *First Thousand Words for Children's Reading*.

WHAT DOES A SCIENTIST DO?

He watches things.

He reads.

He finds out how
things work and
how they can be
made better.

He wonders.

He experiments.

He finds out
what is true.

He sees that
wonderful things
do indeed happen.

I want to be a

SCIENTIST

By Carla Greene
Pictures by Janet LaSalle

Property of
MONROE PUBLIC SCHOOLS

SEP 18 1963
Date_____ No._____

CHILDRENS PRESS, Chicago

Library of Congress Catalog Number: 61-10087

This Edition Printed 1962
Copyright, 1961, Childrens Press
Printed in the U.S.A.

"I wonder what makes a
bean seed grow," said Jack.

"Look at those beans you
are going to plant," said
Sally. "What do you see?"

"I see a white line
and a little black spot."

"Put two of the beans
in water for a few hours,"
said Sally. "Then look
at them again."

The beans that had been
in water were bigger than
the others.

"Why?" asked Jack.

"The little black spot
is a hole," said Sally.
"Water went into the bean
through the hole. Open
the bean. What do you see?"

"I see a baby plant
in the seed," said Jack.
"Yes," said Sally.
"There is some food
for the baby plant in
the seed, too."

Jack planted his beans
in the soft earth.
The sun shone
on his garden.
Rain fell on it.
Jack wondered about
the rain.
"Where does it
come from?" asked Jack.
"Let's find out,"
said Sally.

Sally put some water
in a dish. Soon the
water was gone.
"Water goes into
the air," said Sally.

"Water goes into the
air from lakes, rivers,
oceans, woods and fields."

"I can't see any water
in the air," said Jack.

"I will show you how
to get some water out of
the air. Then you can
see it," said Sally.

Sally put some warm water in a glass.

She put some cold water and ice in another glass.

Water in the air came together in drops on the outside of the cold glass.

"Now I can see some water that was in the air," said Jack.

"But how does water fall as rain?" asked Jack.

Sally said, "Warm air is lighter than cold air. The sun warms the earth and the air near it. The warm air goes up and cool air moves in. As warm air goes high, it cools. Drops of water come together in clouds, as they did on your glass. When the cloud is heavy enough and cool enough, the drops fall as rain."

One day Jack looked
at his garden.

"My beans are growing!"
he cried. "My beans are
growing!"

He looked at the plants.

Each bean plant held up
two little leaves toward
the sun. Jack could see
the two parts of the bean
seed that came up with
the leaves.

"The baby plant in the seed has grown," said Jack. "It has used up the food in the seed. How does it get more food?"

"Let's find out," said Sally.

She got a book.

A green plant needs air, sun, water and good earth.

Water gets plant food from the earth.

Plant roots get the water. The water goes up the stem to the leaves.

The leaves are like little work-shops.

They use water, air and sunshine. They make a kind of sugar that feeds the plant and helps it grow.

Sally folded a paper
towel in half. She put
it around the inside of
a glass.

She soaked some bean
seeds all night. Then
she put them between
the paper and the glass.

She put sand in the
glass. She kept the
sand wet.

The seeds began to grow. Jack could see the roots.

SAND

PAPER TOWEL

People and animals need water, air and sun, too.

But they cannot make their own food as plants do.

People and animals eat plants to get the food that plants make. People also eat animals that eat plants.

People eat big fish that eat little fish that eat the plants in the sea.

One day Jack's bean
plants had long, green
pods on them.

Little beans were
inside of the pods.

Baby plants were
inside of the beans.
"Beans are wonderful,"
said Jack. "I want to
be a scientist and learn
about many things."

At school, Jack told
about his beans.

"Jack is a little
scientist," said his
teacher.

"Am I?" asked Jack.

"Yes. You know how
to look, read and watch.
You see what happens and
try to find out what is
true about the things
around you, even a bean."